Fun Down Under

AUSTRALIA
and
NEW ZEALAND

Caitlyn M. Schmidt

Moonlight Garden Publications

Renton, Washington

No part of this book may be used or reproduced by any means, graphic, electronic, or mechanical, including photocopying, recording, taping or by any information storage retrieval system without the written permission of the publisher, except in the case of brief quotations embodied in critical articles and reviews.

Copyright 2022, Caitlyn M. Schmidt. All rights reserved.

Photography by Caitlyn M. Schmidt (except author portraits and where noted).

Front cover photos taken by Caitlyn M. Schmidt at Sydney Harbor, Sydney, Australia and Hobbiton, Matamata, New Zealand.

Back cover photo taken at Muriwai Beach, Muriwai, New Zealand.

Edited by S. C. Moore.

ISBN: 978-1-938281-49-5 (paperback)
ISBN: 978-1-938281-50-1 (e-book)

Library of Congress Control Number: 2016914379

Published in 2022, Moonlight Garden Publications,
an imprint of Gazebo Gardens Publishing, LLC, Renton, WA
www.GazeboGardensPublishing.com

Printed in the United States of America.

To my parents, who encouraged me
and gave me the incredible opportunity
to fulfill my dreams and desires to
study abroad and to travel.

TABLE OF CONTENTS

1. Introduction — II
2. General Travel Tips — III
   - Sections Color Code Key
3. Australia — 1-27
   - Melbourne (Naarm) — 2-6
     - Day Trips from Melbourne — 7-13
   - Sydney (Warrang) — 14-17
     - Day Trips from Sydney — 18-19
   - Cairns (Gimuy) — 20-21
     - Day Trips from Cairns — 21-23
   - Other Places in Australia — 24-26
   - Aussie Terms — 27
4. New Zealand (Aotearoa) — 28-39
   - Auckland (Tāmaki Makaurau) — 29-32
     - Day Trips from Auckland — 33-35
   - Other Places in New Zealand — 36-38
     - North Island (Te Ika-a-Māui) — 36-37
     - South Island (Te Waipounamu) — 38
   - Kiwi Terms — 39
   - Fiji — 39
5. Website Resource List — 40-45
   - Getting Around — 40
   - Australia Websites — 41-44
   - New Zealand Websites — 44-45
   - Fiji Websites — 45
6. About the Author — 46

INTRODUCTION

As a child, I imagined adventures in faraway lands but never thought those dreams would come true. Yet, as a young adult, I explored castles, visited ruins, and hiked through jungles. Influenced by my dreams to travel and my experiences abroad, I developed an appreciation for the world's countless destinations and cultures and a desire to write about them.

When I was eleven, my parents took me out of the United States for the first time to England, Wales, and Ireland to tour castles, cathedrals, museums, and ancient ruins. When I was fourteen, we ventured to Peru and Bolivia to see Machu Picchu, the Amazon Jungle, and Lake Titicaca. Interacting with new people and exploring fascinating places left me touched and full of wonder.

While attending college, I participated in three academic Study Abroad programs between 2012 and 2013. The first program took me to Australia's east coast and the North Island of New Zealand, with a side trip to Fiji. The second program was in Japan, and the third was in Costa Rica. I have also sojourned in Romania, Hungary, Germany, Austria, the Czech Republic, France, Belgium, the Netherlands, Denmark, Luxembourg, Italy, Spain, and Mexico, and spent a day in Morocco, Gibraltar, and Sweden.

I have gained valuable travel experience over the years and want to share my expertise with others interested in globetrotting. This guidebook gives you a taste of the splendid sights and exciting experiences that await you Down Under. It is compiled from my firsthand experiences, as well as my acquired knowledge and research on Australia and New Zealand.

On the final pages, I have included links for the places and activities described in my book, along with additional websites to help you prepare for your trip. So, no matter where you choose to go, you can use *Fun Down Under* as a savvy resource for sights, excursions, accommodations, restaurants, nightclubs, outdoor activities, cultural considerations, passport and visa requirements, and other helpful tips and tricks to plan your getaway.

General Down Under Travel Tips

Passport validity requirements vary depending on your country of origin. To be safe, be sure your expiry date is at least six months from your projected holiday end. You will also need to check on **travel visa** requirements for the countries you plan to visit, and be sure to have blank pages available at the back of your passport.

For young adult travelers, there are youth hostels in many places throughout Australia and New Zealand. **For backpackers,** look into homestays and vacation rentals, as well as hostels, to find great deals on accommodations.

Before deciding when you want to travel Down Under, be sure to **check what the weather will be like** that time of year. The seasons are opposite from those in North America, Europe, and most of Asia. Summers are very hot, and the sun is strong. Also, check for the latest information regarding any COVID-19 updates or restrictions.

Check online for the **currency exchange rates** before your trip. Be sure to take your debit card to withdraw local currency if needed and your credit card for restaurants, shopping, and activities. Remember to **notify your bank** of your travel itinerary to ensure access to your accounts while abroad.

When hiking through forests, exploring park trails, or visiting beaches in Australia and New Zealand, please be conscious of your impact on the environment. In order to preserve the natural beauty Down Under, make sure you don't leave any garbage or remove things like plants or sand from the ecosystem. It is also important to wipe your shoes clean in parks and forests to prevent the spread of plant diseases that threaten native flora. You may often see trackside cleaning stations for this purpose. Just remember, a small act can have a big impact!

To find links to the websites for sights and activities listed in Fun Down Under, *go to pages 40-45. There are also a number of websites with additional resources to help with preparations for your vacation to Australia, New Zealand, or Fiji. All the included websites were active as of publication in 2022.*

Sections Color Code Key

Color	Section
🟧	General Information
🟨	Countries
🟦	Cities
🟩	Day Trips
🟦	Additional Locations

AUSTRALIA

Melbourne (Naarm)

Melbourne (Naarm) is the capital of the state of Victoria. It is the second largest city in Australia and home to the world's most extensive tram system. The metropolitan area is situated on the rim of Port Phillip Bay (Nerm), into which the Yarra River (Birrarung) runs after winding through a great portion of the city. The roughly 5,000,000 people who live there call themselves Melburnians. Referred to by locals as the Garden City, Melbourne is a huge cultural centre full of shops, museums, and restaurants, as well as a rich nightlife. There are numerous sites in and around Melbourne worth visiting. Whether you enjoy museums and galleries, beaches, shopping, dining, hiking, animal watching, or scenery, you'll find lots to see and do.

Transportation

The easiest way to get around is on the city's Public Transport Victoria system of trams, trains, and buses. If you buy a myki smartcard, you can use any of the three methods to explore the city for a few hours or all day.

Want to fit in with the locals?

When you speak the city's name, avoid the phonetic pronunciation of "Mel-born." Instead, try your Aussie accent on for size, and say "Mel-bun." The locals will be pleased with your effort.

Melbourne Visitor Hub

One of many information centres in the greater Melbourne area, the Melbourne Visitor Hub is located in Melbourne Town Hall on the corner of Little Collins and Swanston streets. Here, you can find all the resources needed for your travels and exploration in the Melbourne area, along with brochures, maps, advice, and assistance with bookings.

Arts Centre Melbourne

Located in the Melbourne Arts Precinct in the central area of the city by the Yarra River, the Arts Centre Melbourne includes multiple performance venues. The tower that conspicuously indicates the location of the complex is composed of a lofty net-like spire with built-in lighting. Nearby, in the Kings Domain parklands, is the Sidney Myer Music Bowl. This outdoor performance area has an impressive 4,055 square metre (43,650 sq. ft.) canopy.

National Gallery of Victoria

The National Gallery of Victoria (NGV) houses contemporary and historic artwork from a range of artists, divided into two sites. The first is The Ian Potter Centre: NGV Australia, located at Federation Square. It is home to the gallery's Australian art, both Indigenous and non-Indigenous, dating from the colonial period to present day. Works include paintings, photography, prints and drawings, sculpture and decorative arts, fashion, textiles, and jewelry. The second gallery is the NGV International at 180 St Kilda Road, which contains the international artwork collections. The majority of the galleries are free to view.

Melbourne Museum

At the Melbourne Museum, you can visit the Bunjilaka Aboriginal Cultural Centre to view an extensive exhibit of Aboriginal art and history. There are numerous rotating exhibits, so make sure to check out what is currently showing in addition to the many that are permanent. These include Dinosaur Walk, The Melbourne Story, The Mind, First Peoples, 600 Million Years, Forest Secrets, Darwin to DNA, Dynamic Earth, and Te Vainui O Pasifika.

University of Melbourne

The University of Melbourne was founded in 1853. It is an internationally recognized, multi-campus institution that offers a wide range of both undergraduate and graduate courses, research programs, and public engagement activities. Historic Newman College, a branch of the university opened in 1918 and designed by renowned architect Walter Griffin, is located at the Parkville campus. The buildings are stunning, from the brick outdoor hallways to the pointed spires. Included on campus are the Academic Centre, the Dining Hall, and the Chapel of the Holy Spirit, shown below. The University of Melbourne welcomes inquiries, and current tour information is available on their website.

Shrine of Remembrance

With its eternal flame, the original purpose of this special shrine was to honor WWII veterans from the state of Victoria. However, the Shrine of Remembrance now stands to memorialize all Australians who served in wartime. The building houses a visitor centre that includes the Hall of Columns, the Gallery of Medals, the Remembrance Garden, an education centre, an audio-visual centre, a gallery space, a retail shop, and a courtyard.

Melbourne Golden Mile Heritage Trail

The Golden Mile Heritage Trail is a fun and unique activity. This walking tour teaches participants how the discovery of gold shaped the city and takes you inside some of Melbourne's historical buildings along the way. If you choose to book the guided tour, it departs from the Melbourne Visitor Centre and takes approximately two hours to complete. You can also opt to follow the round brass discs in the sidewalk on your own, using the Golden Mile booklet that is available for purchase.

Watch for this symbol throughout the city as you walk the trail.

State Library of Victoria

The impressive State Library of Victoria opened in 1856 and today houses over 2,000,000 books. Near the entrance are a pair of bronze lions, as well as statues of Joan of Arc, St. George and the Dragon, and other historical figures. The library's expansive front lawn serves as a popular spot to sit and relax or enjoy your lunch. There's no end to the resources inside; take a tour, and you'll surely be amazed.

www.wikiwand.com/en/State_Library_Victoria

Looking to explore the nightlife?

There are an abundance of clubs and bars to enjoy in Melbourne if you are looking to mingle, dance, or simply enjoy a drink. Don't miss out on some of the most popular places to spend the evening: La Di Da, The Toff in Town, and Rooftop Bar.

TRAVEL TIP

To protect your passport, cards, and cash, consider purchasing a crossbody theft-proof bag and an RFID wallet or money belt to prevent credit card and ID theft during your travels.

Day Trips from Melbourne

Outside the city, you'll find breathtaking scenery with beaches, wildlife sanctuaries, and numerous excursions to choose from. Although it's possible to take the "self tour" option, if you'd prefer to make bookings ahead of time, many tours should be available through your hotel, as well as the Melbourne Visitor Hub and local travel agencies.

St Kilda (Euro Yuroke)

Be sure to make a day trip down to St Kilda (Euro Yuroke), a suburb of Melbourne's metropolitan area. In addition to sand and surf, you can visit the promenade, harbour, pier, sea baths, marine clubs, and restaurants there. Or, if you like to be active, try roller blading, windsurfing, paddle boarding, swimming, sailing, kite-surfing, boating, skydiving, snorkeling, or jet skiing. There are also plenty of bars and a vibrant nightlife to enjoy in the area. While in St Kilda, be sure to spend some time at the most famous sandy spot in Melbourne, St Kilda Beach on Port Phillip Bay.

Luna Park

Situated above St Kilda Beach, Luna Park overlooks Port Phillip Bay. In 2012, the amusement park proudly celebrated 100 years of fun and history. Today, it offers attractions for people of all ages, including a wide variety of rides. The park's wooden Great Scenic Railway is the oldest continually operating roller coaster in the world.

Great Ocean Road

Drive 245 kilometres (152 mi.) southwest of Melbourne to experience the Great Ocean Road. Along the route, view the spectacular coastline with unusual and breathtaking rock formations in Port Campbell National Park, like the Twelve Apostles, Gibson Steps, Loch Ard Gorge, Thunder Cave, The Grotto, and London Bridge. There are also rivers, rainforests, volcanoes, and wildlife at the Tower Hill State Game Reserve. In addition, the route passes by a wine region and the town of Geelong, where you can learn about the Aboriginal culture.

www.complexmania.com/great-ocean-road/

Phillip Island (Millowl) Fairy Penguins

In just under two hours from Melbourne, you can drive or bus to Summerland Beach at the southern tip of Phillip Island (Millowl) to view the fairy penguin parade. At dusk, the little creatures arrive home by the hundreds after a day at sea to rest for the night in the sand dunes. They waddle past in groups, sometimes in single file, for nearly an hour. Please keep in mind that photography is not allowed, as sounds and flashes from phones or cameras may frighten the tiny penguins. Be sure to book your viewing ahead of time at the Melbourne Visitor Centre, at your hotel, or through the Phillip Island website. There are numerous viewing options, so take a look at each ticket description before picking the experience that fits your preferences and budget the best.

Maru Koala and Animal Park

As they say at Maru Koala and Animal Park, "get in touch with wildlife" while visiting this family friendly attraction. The enjoyable exhibits feature a variety of Australian animals that you can view, feed, and in some cases, even pet! Also for your entertainment, there's an eighteen-hole miniature golf course, a bistro, an indoor playroom, a gift shop, a professional photography booth for photos with the animals, and an auditorium that features daily shows.

Bendigo

In the gold rush town of Bendigo, just a ninety-minute drive northwest of Melbourne, you can visit many cultural and historic sites. Explore the Soldiers Memorial Museum, go down in an old gold mine, visit the 1860s Chinese Joss House, or take the Vintage Talking Tram  tour. Walk through the Bendigo Art Gallery, make your own pottery, take a stroll through Whipstick Forest, or ride Australia's highest vertical slide at the Discovery Science & Technology Centre. Don't miss the beautifully decorated Golden Dragon Museum to see Sun Loong, the world's longest Imperial Dragon, and the lovely gardens near the entrance, pictured here.

Balbirooroo Wetlands

The Balbirooroo Wetlands Walk is a trail that runs through the Balbirooroo Wetlands, an area located about 64.4 kilometres (40 mi.) south of Melbourne on Mornington Peninsula. There are information boards, viewing platforms, and many places to observe the wetland flora and fauna. As you explore the area, watch for a variety of birds, including chestnut teals, ducks, egrets, cormorants, and the majestic black swan.

Healesville Sanctuary

At the Healesville Sanctuary, just over an hour's drive east of Melbourne, view Australian wildlife in natural-style habitats. You'll see Tasmanian devils, koalas, wallabies, emus, platypus, dingoes, wombats, echidnas, and a variety of reptiles. You may even get to pet the dingoes if they happen to be out on a walk through the sanctuary. Make sure to stick around for the fascinating Spirit of the Sky bird show, and, of course, don't leave without petting the kangaroos!

Mornington Peninsula National Park

Just over an hour's drive south of Melbourne is Cape Schanck in Mornington Peninsula National Park. You'll find beaches, tide pools, scenic trails, and ocean views. Formations like the rounded Pulpit Rock and the flat area surrounding it called Devil's Desk, pictured below, can be seen from a lookout. While exploring the trails, you might catch a glimpse of an echidna in its natural habitat—if you're lucky! There's also a lighthouse, a museum, and the former lighthouse keeper's cottage, which was constructed in 1859. Fees apply to view the lighthouse buildings.

Bushrangers Bay

The drive to Bushrangers Bay from the city offers lovely coastal scenery. This large beach park south of Melbourne features a number of walking trails and a beach surrounded by breathtaking basalt cliffs.

Yarra Ranges National Park

Located in the Yarra Ranges National Park, just over 80.5 kilometres (50 mi.) east of Melbourne, is Mount Donna Buang summit, a local favorite area for hiking, biking, and picnics. The nearly 21.3 metre (70 ft.) tall observation tower there offers spectacular panoramas of Melbourne, Mount Baw Baw and the Alps, the Dandenong and Cathedral Ranges, and the Yarra Valley. On the Donna Buang mountainside, you can visit the Rainforest Gallery. At this site, there's a raised observation platform that's 15 metres (49 ft.) above the ground for viewing the rainforest canopy. Be sure to walk the gorgeous 350-metre (1,148-ft.) walkway that winds down through the rainforest to the gully below.

www.visitmelbourne.com/Regions/Yarra-Valley-and-Dandenong-Ranges/

TRAVEL TIP

Always take water, sunscreen, sunglasses, and a hat along with you for any outdoor activity. The sun is harsh Down Under. Plan to wear comfortable walking shoes, as hiking trails can be lengthy and uneven. It's also a good idea to bring some snacks in case there's a long time between meals.

Sydney (Warrang)

Situated on the coast of the Tasman Sea in southeast Australia, Sydney (Warrang) is the capital of the state of New South Wales and is renowned for its architecture, parks and open spaces, festivals, and cultural attractions. It is Australia's largest city, with a population of over 5,000,000 people, and the locals call themselves Sydneysiders.

Transportation

Sydney's public transport system is comprised of train, bus, and ferry services. The Opal Card is the smartcard ticket to load funds on to get around the city, and it includes the light rail for traveling to outlying areas and regions.

Sydney Visitor Centre

One of several visitor centres and kiosks in the greater Sydney area, The Rocks Centre location has many services available. These include bookings for accommodations, tours and attractions, interstate and countrywide flights, and discounted attraction passes. The knowledgeable staff can provide tips, free information, and maps.

Sydney Harbour

Surrounded by miles of beautiful shoreline, historic sites, and national parks, Sydney Harbour is part of Port Jackson and is one of the largest natural harbours in the world. Take a ride on the Sydney Ferry to experience the beauty of the harbour. You'll see the world-famous Sydney Opera House, the impressive Sydney Harbour Bridge, and over half a dozen islands, some with convict-built structures and forts, and others rich with Aboriginal history.

Sydney Opera House

The late-modern architecture of the Sydney Opera House is an impressive sight to behold. It's a world-class performing arts centre, and there are always numerous shows playing. When touring this World Heritage Site, make sure to look at the schedule for these amazing performances.

Sydney Harbour Bridge

A national landmark, the Sydney Harbour Bridge is 134 metres (440 ft.) at its highest point. Four different climbs are available during the day for a variety of views from dawn to dark. Several million people have climbed to the bridge's summit. If you don't want to do the bridge climb, you can walk along the pedestrian path for a brilliant view of the harbour and the Sydney Opera House.

Fort Denison – Muddawahnyuh

On one of Sydney Harbour's small islands called Muddawahnyuh, stands Fort Denison, completed in 1857. This historic site has served a variety of functions from colonial times to the present day. Guided tours include access to a museum and the unique Martello Tower. Following tradition, the one o'clock cannon is fired daily, just as it was from 1906 to 1942 when it was used by sailors to set their chronometers to the local time.

Taronga Zoo

There's always something fun to do at Taronga Zoo, on the north side of Sydney Harbour. With over 4,000 animals to view, keeper talks and shows, tours, events, and concerts, you'll have a wonderful day there.

Royal Botanic Garden Sydney

Right at the edge of Sydney Harbour, wrapped around Farm Cove, lies 30 hectares (74 acres) of tranquility in the Royal Botanic Garden Sydney. Established in 1816, the site has a rich history and offers plenty to see and do for visitors of all ages. You won't regret exploring this bit of paradise in the heart of the city.

SEA LIFE Sydney Aquarium

Step into Australia's underwater world and observe the animals that live in its freshwater and marine aquatic environments. At SEA LIFE Sydney Aquarium, you'll see penguins, sharks, stingrays, dugongs, sawfish, thousands of tropical fish, and many other creatures of the deep.

Hyde Park and St Mary's Cathedral

Hyde Park is filled with lush grassy areas, big, leafy trees, and plenty of benches. It is the oldest park in Australia and an ideal place to relax in the city's centre. One of Sydney's loveliest fountains, Archibald Fountain, sits at the north end of the park, right across from St Mary's Cathedral. This English-style Gothic Catholic church is one of the city's grand historic buildings and was constructed from local limestone.

Looking to explore the nightlife?

Many of Sydney's top nightclubs are in Darlinghurst, Surry Hills, and the Central Business District. King Street Wharf and The Rocks is where you'll find more upscale bars and clubs, some with views of the harbor. Check out the historic three-level 3 Wise Monkeys in Haymarket. Each floor serves a different function: pub dining, cocktail lounge, and late-night parties and entertainment.

Day Trips from Sydney

A number of interesting and scenic day trips can be taken from Sydney. Below are just a few suggestions.

Manly (Canna)

A northern suburb of Sydney, the area known as Manly (Canna) is the gateway to the Northern Beaches. It is the perfect spot for shopping, dining, walks, views, galleries, museums, and other activities.

www.arcadiala.com.au/urbantexture-when-urban-design-meets-landscape-architecture/

Bondi Beach (Boondi)

In a suburb of Sydney, Bondi (Boondi) is one of Australia's most famous beaches. This white, sandy stretch is nearly 1 kilometre (over 3,200 ft.) long and is patrolled by lifeguards for your swimming enjoyment.

www.janameerman.com/bondi-to-coogee/

Australian Reptile Park

The Australian Reptile Park, an hour's drive north of Sydney, is home to birds, reptiles, amphibians, spiders, and mammals, mostly from Australia, as well as some
www.weekendnotes.com/australian-reptile-park/34313
from around the world. Animal interaction, wildlife shows, and exhibits abound in this award-winning hands-on zoo.

Hunter Valley

Just a two-hour drive north of Sydney is Hunter Valley. This is wine country, and tours are available to visit the many local wineries. While you're in the area, be sure to check out Hunter Valley Gardens, a collection of shops, restaurants, cafés, and rides nestled in an exquisitely landscaped, extensive garden. Accommodations from studio rooms to suites are also available there. In addition, the heritage-listed Baiame Cave is nearby, which is home to Aboriginal rock art dating back thousands of years.

Blue Mountains National Park

A two-hour drive west of Sydney is the World Heritage Blue Mountains National Park noted for its breathtaking views, including the Three Sisters rock formation of Aboriginal legend. Nearby is the historic town of Katoomba and the adventure park, Scenic World, where you can ride the Scenic Railway to an ancient rainforest. Also close by are the Jenolan Caves (Binoomea), filled with limestone formations. Accommodations for caves tours include the Caves House, a Tudor-style building from the Victorian era also listed with World Heritage.

Cairns (Gimuy)

Cairns (Gimuy) is a city of less than 200,000 people at the north end of Queensland, Australia. It is a seaport, and with its tropical climate and proximity to the Great Barrier Reef, it's a popular location for international tourists to enjoy the scenery and water sports. There are also plenty of shopping areas, restaurants, and bars.

Transportation

The Cairns public transportation system is comprised of a bus service that runs from City Place to locations all over the city, including the Northern Beaches.

Reef Info Visitor Information Centre

Located at Shop 1, 34 The Esplanade, this accredited visitor information centre offers resources including maps, brochures, and itineraries. Staffed by knowledgeable locals, the centre can provide advice on things to see and do, places to eat, and travel tips for Cairns.

The Esplanade

The Esplanade is defined by its impressive saltwater "lagoon" public pool overlooking the Great Barrier Reef. You'll also find food, shopping, and live entertainment in the area. Play in the sand, sunbathe, or sit in the beautifully landscaped gardens.

www.cairnsaccommodation.com

Want to fit in with the locals?

Avoid the phonetic pronunciation of "Care-ns," and try it the Aussie way. Say "Cans," and locals will be impressed.

Looking to explore the nightlife?

There's a rich nightlife culture in Cairns, and many of the establishments are within walking distance from the main part of town. Don't miss out on my favorite party places: The Woolshed, Gilligan's with its three bars, and The Attic Lounge Bar.

Day Trips from Cairns

There is much to do just outside of this lively tourist city. Find your sense of adventure and explore the jungle, zipline through the trees, or paddle on the rivers. Whatever you choose, it's certain that you'll not only enjoy your excursions, but the scenery as well.

Fitzroy Island (Koba or Gabar)

If you want to explore the Great Barrier Reef, consider a trip to Fitzroy Island (Koba or Gabar) or booking a stay at the Fitzroy Island Resort. There are multiple tour and rental options, including sea kayaking, snorkeling, paddleboarding, and glass bottom boats. Some day trips include a scenic catamaran ride to the island, guided activities, and picnic lunch. Fitzroy Island Dive Center offers both introductory and certified diving. There is also the Cairns Turtle Rehabilitation Centre where you can visit the turtles by booking a tour.

Cape Tribulation (Kurangee)

Take a drive up the coast to Port Douglas (Diju), under two hours from Cairns, and on north to Cape Tribulation (Kurangee). This is where the Great Barrier Reef meets the rainforest. You can go horseback riding on the beach at the cape, go snorkeling or kayaking in the clear blue water, or take a relaxing stroll along the beach.

Daintree

Ride a riverboat into the Daintree Rainforest and stay at a lodge or hostel in the Daintree region. If you're lucky, you might see some crocodiles in the river on your way upstream. While there, you can go on guided walks to see the flora and fauna, go ziplining, or experience the activities at Daintree Discovery Centre. These include the Daintree Rainforest Aerial Walkway, the Canopy Tower, and the Interpretive Display Centre.

www.luxurylodgesofaustralia.com

Skypark Cairns by AJ Hackett

Skypark Cairns by AJ Hackett will attract adventurous travelers. It has the only Bungy Tower and Giant Jungle Swing in Australia, as well as the recently added Walk the Plank activity with extensive views of the ocean and rainforest. If you bungy jump, you have the option to take a refreshing dip in the water below. They also record your experience and offer a video for purchase so you'll have proof for your family and friends!

Tully River (Balan Jaban) White Water Rafting

Take a white water rafting ride on the Tully River (Balan Jaban) with Raging Thunder Adventures, the company who's been doing commercial tours since 1984. All equipment is provided, no experience is needed, and their highly qualified guides teach safety measures to your rowing team before the trip downriver begins. The excursion also includes lunch on the riverside. Just bring your swimsuit (or clothing you don't mind getting wet), a towel, secure shoes, sunscreen, bug spray, and money to purchase the great professional pictures they capture of your rafting outing, like the one below. It makes for quite the thrilling day!

Photo used with permission from Raging Thunder Adventures

Crystal Cascades

Go exploring with Cairns Canyoning at the Crystal Cascades waterfalls in the Cairns rainforest. While there, you'll zipline, rappel sheer rock faces, slide down natural rock slides, swim, traverse the gorges and rainforest, and leap beside waterfalls cascading into pools. You might see wildlife such as: lizards, snakes, birds, and vivid butterflies and dragonflies. This day trip includes transportation from central Cairns, all necessary equipment, and training from qualified guides. Make sure to bring sunscreen, a snack, a towel and a change of clothes, and money to purchase photos or videos of your excursion.

Other Places in Australia

Coober Pedy (Umoona) is known as the opal capital of the world. This semitransparent gemstone was first discovered there in 1915, and today, nearly 70% of the world's opal is found in Coober Pedy. Most of the town and the locals' homes are underground in this desert Outback location, along with churches, shopping, and mining. The cosmopolitan town is home to a multicultural population of forty-five nationalities and is one of the most unique places in Australia. Plan to spend at least two days there to see the sights.

www.realestate.com.au/lifestyle/living-underground

Alice Springs (Mparntwe) is the gateway to the Outback's Red Centre, where you can visit the sandstone monolith, Uluru / Ayers Rock, one of the most impressive landmarks in Australia. Also in the area is the striking landscape of Kata Tjuta / Mount Olga, Tjoritja / West MacDonnell Ranges, and the Watarrka National Park with fascinating locations such as Kings Canyon and the Garden of Eden.

www.crystalinks.com/ayersrock

Darwin (Garramilla) is the capital of the Northern Territory, and there is plenty to see and do in and around the city. Take a jumping crocodile cruise, see wetlands and reserves, take an Aboriginal cultural tour, enjoy a fishing charter trip, or swim at Berry Springs in crystal clear waterholes. Head to the suburb of Nightcliff to indulge in the rich bar and restaurant scene, or explore the largest national park in Australia, Kakadu National Park. Within the park at Nourlangie, Nanguluwur, and Ubirr, you can view Aboriginal rock paintings dating back to prehistoric times.

www.aussieadventurecamping.wordpress.com

Perth (Boorloo), situated on the southwest coast, is the capital of Western Australia. Explore the parks and beaches, visit the Margaret River (Wooditchup) wine region, go to Rottnest Island (Wadjemup) to see quokkas—marsupials related to kangaroos and wallabies—or view the striking limestone formations in Nambung National Park called the Pinnacles. There are also many cultural activities available.

www.familypedia.wikia.com/wiki/Perth

Adelaide (Tarndanya) is South Australia's coastal capital, and the city's South Australia Museum is devoted to natural history. You can go to the park or the beach, swim with dolphins, go on a drive to visit nearby wineries, or take a trip to Kangaroo Island (Karta Pintingga). From Adelaide, you can also take a cross-country train up to Darwin at the top of Australia and see the variety of scenery the region has to offer.

Canberra (Ngambri Ngunnawal), the capital of Australia, is surrounded by park lands and native bushland. There are museums, galleries, seasonal festivals, and lakes for water sports. Plus, the Australian Alps and national parks and reserves are a short drive away.

Brisbane (Meanjin), the capital of Queensland, is home to the Queensland Museum and numerous other galleries and museums. Atop Mount Coot-tha, which looms over the city and provides panoramic views, you'll find the Brisbane Botanic Gardens and the Summit Lookout facilities. The Sunshine Coast (Kabi Kabi), with its popular beaches for surfing or swimming, is just over an hour away from the city. Visit the Lone Pine Koala Sanctuary, go on a whale watching cruise, take a bike ride, or climb the Brisbane Story Bridge.

www.experienceoz.com.au

Tasmania (Lutruwita), nicknamed Tassie, is an island Commonwealth State of Australia off the mainland's southern coastline. Nearly 45% of the island is comprised of reserves, national parks, and World Heritage sites. There are many places to visit, including The Blade at Cape Pillar, The Bay of Fires (Larapuna), Blue Tier Forest Reserve, Freycinet Peninsula, Port Arthur, the city of Hobart, and Horseshoe Falls.

www.bestworldtourism.com

Here are a few terms for your time in Australia:

Aboriginal peoples and Torres Strait Islander peoples – also known as the First Peoples and the Traditional Owners of the lands; the Indigenous people of Australia, made up of many cultures, traditions, languages, and histories

Terminology for peoples and individuals varies across the country. If you're unsure what term to use, you may want to ask politely about regional or personal preference. For more information, a helpful starting point is:

teaching.unsw.edu.au/indigenous-terminology

Aussie or Ozzie – Australian
Bloke – man, guy
Brekkie – breakfast
Coldie – a beer
Down Under – Australia and New Zealand
G'day – hello
Hooroo – goodbye
Lollies – sweets, candy
Mate – buddy, friend
Never Never – the Outback, centre of Australia
No worries – expression of reassurance; no problem
Outback – interior of Australia
Oz – Australia
Sheila – woman, gal
Sunnies – sunglasses
Top End – far north of Australia

NEW ZEALAND (AOTEAROA)

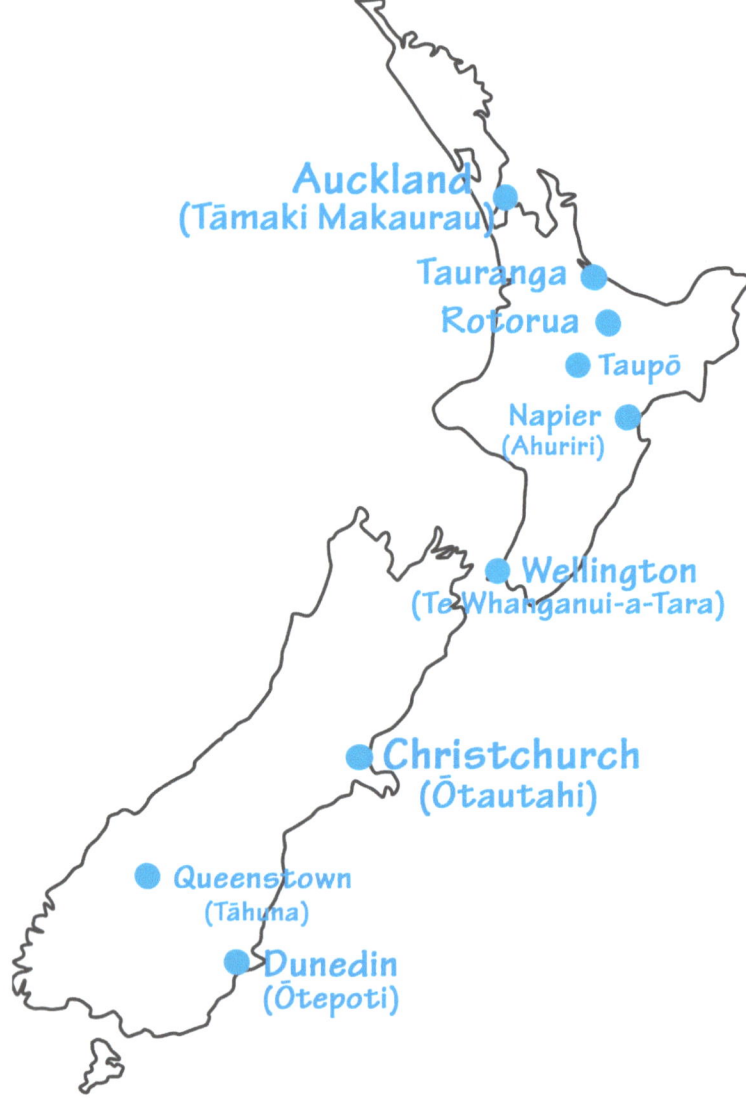

Auckland (Tāmaki Makaurau)

Auckland (Tāmaki Makaurau) is located on the North Island (Te Ika-a-Māui) of New Zealand (Aotearoa) on the Hauraki Gulf (Tīkapa Moana o Hauraki) in the South Pacific Ocean (Te Moana-nui-a-Kiwa). It is the country's largest metropolitan area with roughly 1,650,000 residents, including the world's largest population of Polynesians in a single city. There are plenty of shopping centres, restaurants, museums, and cultural centres, as well as an energetic nightlife.

Transportation

Pick up an AT HOP prepay card for use on the bus, train, and ferry public transportation system to get around and see all the sights.

SkyCity i-SITE Visitor Information Centre

Located on the corner of Victoria and Federal streets, SkyCity i-SITE is one of the official visitor centres in the Auckland area that offer free information, advice, and activity and travel bookings. Some also sell gifts and souvenirs.

Sky Tower and SkyCity

Ride a glass-front elevator to the top of the Sky Tower, New Zealand's tallest man-made structure, and watch Auckland shrink below you. Facilities inside this 328-metre (1,076-ft.) structure include: a café, observation levels, the rotating Orbit restaurant, The Sugar Club restaurant, and the thrilling SkyJump and SkyWalk attractions. The Sky Tower is part of a two-block entertainment complex in central Auckland called SkyCity. Aside from bars and restaurants, there are three hotels, a casino, a theatre, and a convention centre.

Auckland War Memorial Museum
Tāmaki Paenga Hira

The historic Auckland War Memorial Museum Tāmaki Paenga Hira, commonly known as the Auckland Museum, is home to the world's largest Māori and Pacific Island collection and also serves as the province's war memorial. Included in the cultural exhibits and artifacts is an 1870s storehouse along with weapons, tools, carvings, and animal skeletons. There is also an impressive wharenui, or Māori meetinghouse, built in 1878. When you enter this sacred area, be sure to remove your shoes according to custom. In addition, the museum contains decorative arts and natural, social, and military history collections, as well as a library, galleries, and exhibitions.

Maungakiekie / One Tree Hill

Maungakiekie / One Tree Hill is a volcanic cone and historic Māori settlement complex. In addition to the former fortified settlement and terracing, you can enjoy breathtaking views of the city. Below the summit of this dormant volcano lie three craters, a field of volcanic rock, and open grassy fields. The band U2 released a song about One Tree Hill in 1988, which in turn inspired the 2003 television drama series of the same name.

Want to fit in with the locals?

Use the expression "sweet as." In New Zealand, this phrase has multiple meanings. It can be a substitution for "good" or "cool," as well as an affirmative statement in the place of "yes," "right," or "okay." It's also used as a descriptive phrase, such as, "The waves were *sweet as* when we were surfing today!"

Maungawhau / Mount Eden

From the top of Maungawhau / Mount Eden, an extinct volcano and the highest point in Auckland, you have a 360-degree view of the city and its surrounding areas. This landmark is recorded in traditional Māori myths, and ceremonies were held for the deity Mataaho in its 50 metre (164 ft.) deep crater. Trendy cafés and wine bars line Mount Eden Road, as well as bookshops and vintage clothing stores.

Cathedral of St Patrick & St Joseph

The Cathedral of St Patrick and St Joseph, located in Auckland's city centre, was founded in 1841. It was fully remodeled in 2007, maintaining its Gothic Revival style. Inside the tower are the oldest bells in New Zealand, cast in Rome in 1723 and brought to the cathedral in 1884. The church has Belgian stained glass windows and polished wood on the altar, and in the old confessional on the left, there is a historical display. Outside is St Patrick's Square, an oasis in which to rest and relax in the busy city.

www.minikiwiland.co.nz/info.

Auckland Bridge Bungy Jump and Climb

For a true New Zealand adventure, book a bungy jump off the Auckland Harbour Bridge with AJ Hackett Bungy. Enjoy incredible views of Waitematā Harbour during the exclusive bridge walk that takes you out to the jump platform. You can even choose to do a flip to take the plunge, or take an ocean dip during your jump—how refreshing! If you'd prefer to enjoy the view with your feet firmly planted, try the AJ Hackett bridge climb instead. This guided tour not only takes you to the bridge's summit, but offers an easy walkway to get there. Both the bungy jump and bridge climb have photo and video options to chronicle your experience.

www.aucklandscenictours.co.nz/gallery/

Looking to explore the nightlife?

There are many fun places to go to enjoy the night in the city. Whether you like clubs or bars, dancing or meeting new people, don't miss out on the fun. One of my favorite spots in Auckland is LaZeppa Kitchen & Bar.

TRAVEL TIP

Tipping servers in restaurants is not expected in New Zealand. But, just like in Australia, if your server does an exceptional job, feel free to leave a 10% tip. It will be appreciated.

Day Trips from Auckland

Wonderful excursions within a couple hours of the city are available, including Hobbiton, where filming of the Shire from *The Lord of the Rings* and *The Hobbit* trilogies took place.

Hobbiton

On rolling farmland just outside the town of Matamata, only two hours southeast of Auckland, lies the setting for the Shire, a piece of J.R.R. Tolkien's Middle-earth. The movie set was originally constructed for the filming of *The Lord of the Rings* trilogy but was subsequently refurbished for *The Hobbit: An Unexpected Journey*. Fans will love the natural setting as they walk through Hobbiton. Visit the Party Tree, the outside of Bilbo Baggins' hobbit hole, the lake, the bridge, and the Green Dragon Inn—where you can sit inside and enjoy food and drink. There are a number of tour options to choose from, and facilities on-site include a souvenir shop and a cafe.

Waitakere Ranges Regional Park

On New Zealand's western coastline, just a thirty-minute drive from Auckland, lies the expansive Waitakere Ranges Regional Park. This forest is home to numerous waterfalls, rivers, beaches, bird species, giant kauri trees, and historic homesteads. Stop at the Arataki Visitor Centre to find information on park facilities and the many wonderful walking trails. Activities at Waitakere Ranges park include hiking, camping, boating, fishing, and surfing.

Muriwai Beach

Thirty-five minutes due west of Auckland lies this black sand beach, a famous spot for surfing, swimming, and fishing. Muriwai Beach is home to one of New Zealand's only mainland gannet breeding colonies, the Takapu Refuge. These seabirds nest along the coastline between August and March yearly. If you visit to enjoy the elegant volcanic black sand, you can sunbathe or take a stroll along the beach. Don't forget to explore the rock platform that overlooks the beach—but watch out for the giant waves that splash high and without warning!

Piha Beach

www.pxhere.com/en/photo/838627

The most famous surfing beach in New Zealand, Piha Beach, is only 40 kilometres (25 mi.) west of Auckland. Also referred to as one of the most dangerous beaches, Piha often has rough, wind-swept waves from the Tasman Sea (Te Tai-o-Rēhua) rolling onto its black sand shore.

Tiritiri Matangi Open Sanctuary

Buy your tickets in advance to ensure a visit to the Tiritiri Matangi Island wildlife sanctuary, located 30 kilometres (18.6 mi.) northeast of Auckland. To create this sanctuary, the island's former farmland was reforested, and all natural predators were removed to make a home for threatened and endangered birds, reptiles, and other wildlife. Tiritiri Matangi is accessible by ferry and has a lighthouse, a beach, and a Visitor Centre with beverages available for purchase—but remember to pack your own lunch. If you'd like to go on a night walk for a chance to see New Zealand's nocturnal national symbol, the kiwi bird, you can book a room at the bunkhouse in the former lighthouse keeper's cottage.

Waitomo Caves

A spelunker's paradise awaits you at Waitomo Caves, less than two and a half hours south of Auckland. Guided tours through a series of three main cave systems, full of indigenous glowworms and natural formations, include an oral history and an explanation of the fascinating geology of these caves. The exploration begins with the Waitomo Glowworm Caves by boat or inner tube. Next, Ruakuri Cave hosts New Zealand's longest underground guided walking tour. Last is Aranui Cave with stalagmites, stalactites, flowstones, and a colony of cricket-like insects called cave weta.

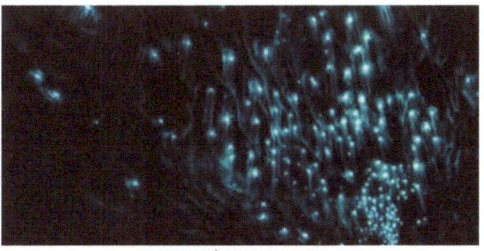

www.waitomocaves.com

Other Places in New Zealand: North Island (Te Ika-a-Māui)

Wellington (Te Whanganui-a-Tara) is the capital of New Zealand and lies on the coast near the southernmost point of the North Island, overlooking Cook Strait (Raukawa Moana). Ride the red cable car to Wellington Botanic Garden, walk along the waterfront promenade, relax on one of the beaches, and visit the zoo or a museum.

www.traveller.com.au/wellington

www.runnersworldonline.com.au/event/tauranga-international-marathon/

Tauranga, located on the Bay of Plenty, (Te Moana-a-Toi) has activities galore and many places to explore. All types of water sports are available, beautiful beaches lie nearby, and there are shops, galleries, and The Strand for a variety of restaurants and clubs. The area also has several hiking trails, waterfalls, and sanctuaries.

Taupō sits at the edge of Lake Taupō (Taupō-nui-a-Tia), the largest lake in the region of Australasia. Fishing, skiing, hiking, lake cruises, kayak expeditions, cycling, geothermal walks, and golfing are just some of the activities available. The magnificent Huka Falls (Hukanui) is just north of the lake, and at the valley, Craters of the Moon (Karapiti), you can view cauldrons of boiling mud.

www.trover.com/d/1BUHZ-huka-falls-wairakei-new-zealand

Rotorua sits on Lake Rotorua / Te Rotorua nui ā Kahumatamomoe and is noted for its mudpools, geysers, hot springs, and renowned mountain bike trails that zigzag through its lush forests. Rotorua is home to Te Puia, a 70-hectare (173-acre) area that includes the New Zealand Māori Arts and Crafts Institute, established to educate the public and preserve the culture and traditional arts of the Māori people. Don't miss out on Te Puia's geothermal valley, the Kiwi Conservation Centre, the Māori village, and the craftspeople at work. Tickets are available for daily guided tours, and don't miss the Te Puia Store with Māori-crafted décor, gifts, and souvenirs.

www.go4travelblog.com/orakei-korako-cave-craters-of-the-moon/

Napier (Ahuriri), on the coast of the Hawke's Bay (Te Matau-a-Māui) region, was destroyed by a 7.9 earthquake and local fires in 1931. When it was rebuilt, it was done so in the architectural styles of the day: stripped classical, Spanish mission, and art deco. During construction, Māori motifs were incorporated in the design of a select few buildings. Enjoy the architecture, view the gannet colony at Cape Kidnappers (Te Kauwae-a-Māui), and visit some vineyards.

www.teara.govt.nz/en/photograph/5824/cape-kidnappers-colony

Other Places in New Zealand: South Island (Te Waipounamu)

Christchurch (Ōtautahi), known as the Garden City, is on the east coast of New Zealand's South Island. From there, you can ski, bungy jump, river raft, mountain bike, surf, swim, golf, or view dolphins, whales, and seals. Take a hot air balloon ride to get a fabulous view of the mountains and the Pacific Ocean. Be sure to visit a sheep farm while in the area.

www.stuff.co.nz/travel/destinations/nz/94618674/six-of-the-best-australia-and-new-zealand-mountain-drives

Queenstown (Tāhuna), located inland on the shore of Lake Wakatipu (Whakatipu wai-māori), beneath the majestic Remarkables mountain range (Kawarau), is the world capital of bungy jumping and year-round water sports. You can visit local wineries or the historic mining town of Arrowtown (Haehaenui), ride a gondola, fish for trout, or bungy jump off of Kawarau Gorge Suspension Bridge.

www.new-zealand-travel-showcase.com/queenstown-activities

Dunedin (Ōtepoti) is the oldest city in New Zealand and sits on the edge of Otago Harbour (Wai Ōtākou) on the southeast coast. The city is known for its Victorian and Edwardian architecture and its Māori and Scottish heritage. The Otago Peninsula's (Muaūpoko) rugged landscape is home to penguins, albatrosses, sea lions, seals, and the country's only castle, Larnach Castle, which was built in 1871.

www.larnachcastle.co.nz

Here are a few terms for your time in New Zealand:

Aotearoa – New Zealand (Māori language)
Biscuits – cookies
Bloke – man
Cheers – thanks, goodbye
Chick – woman
Down Under – New Zealand and Australia
Gidday – hello
Godzone – New Zealand
Handle – pint of beer
Jar – glass of beer
Kia ora – hello (Māori language)
Kiwi – New Zealander
Mate – buddy, friend
Māori – the indigenous people of New Zealand; the culture made up of the Māori language, traditions, and history
No worries – no problem
Sunnies – sunglasses
Sweet as – cool, or something really good

Fiji

While in New Zealand, consider a side trip to Fiji. For the best deals, travel to the islands between the months of November and April. There are over fifty resorts and hotels spread across approximately 330 islands, many of which are on the two largest islands, Viti Levu and Vanua Levu. Resort facilities vary greatly, so do your homework before choosing your destination. A great option is Beachcomber Island Resort, a small island encircled by a white beach, exclusive to resort guests, and managed by the cheerful and welcoming staff. Play or relax by day, and party through the night in your choice of accommodations. You may also have the opportunity to try the traditional kava root drink. Expect to frequently hear *bula* (a greeting or blessing that translates to "life") and *vinaka* (meaning "thank you") from the friendly locals!

Getting Around Australia, New Zealand, and Fiji

Australia is a large country and can be easiest to get around by air. However, there are also some train routes that afford beautiful scenery and side trips. Or, you can take a bus or rent a vehicle and drive around parts of the country at your own pace.

www.australia.com/en-us/facts-and-planning/getting-around.html
www.railmaps.com.au
www.australiatrains.com/train-routes.html
www.australian-trains.com/ghan
www.australia.com/en-us/trips-and-itineraries/best-road-trips-australia.html

Tasmania is a small island easily navigated by the local bus system, rental car, or taxi/rideshare.

www.discovertasmania.com.au/planning/getting-around/

New Zealand is a small country, and the North and South islands are connected by ferry, making it easy to explore them both without having to fly. If you want to enjoy more of the scenery, your travel options include trains or buses, or you can rent a vehicle and drive from one end of the country to the other.

www.newzealand.com/us/getting-around
www.newzealand.com/us/rail/
www.newzealand.com/us/trips-and-driving-itineraries/
www.newzealand.com/us/driving-in-new-zealand/

Fiji covers roughly 18,000 square kilometres (7,000 sq. mi.). You can fly, drive, or cruise to get around the expansive country.

www.fiji.travel/articles/getting-around-fiji
www.fijipocketguide.com/7-ways-to-get-around-fiji/

AUSTRALIA

Melbourne (Naarm)
Transportation
www.ptv.vic.gov.au
Melbourne Visitor Hub
whatson.melbourne.vic.gov.au/visitor-info/visitor-centres/melbourne-visitor-hub
Arts Centre Melbourne
www.artscentremelbourne.com.au
National Gallery of Victoria
www.ngv.vic.gov.au
Melbourne Museum
www.museumsvictoria.com.au/melbournemuseum/
University of Melbourne
www.unimelb.edu.au/contact   https://study.unimelb.edu.au/discover/virtual-tour
Shrine of Remembrance
www.shrine.org.au/
Melbourne Golden Mile Heritage Trail
www.hiddensecretstours.com/tour/golden-mile/
State Library of Victoria
www.slv.vic.gov.au
Looking to explore the nightlife?
www.traveltriangle.com/blog/best-nightlife-in-melbourne/

Day Trips from Melbourne
www.timeout.com/melbourne/travel/the-best-day-trips-from-melbourne
www.railmaps.com.au/melbournedaytrips.htm
St Kilda (Euro Yuroke)
www.travelvictoria.com.au/stkilda/
www.stkildamelbourne.com.au
Luna Park
www.lunapark.com.au
Great Ocean Road
www.visitvictoria.com/Regions/great-ocean-road
Phillip Island (Millowl) Fairy Penguins
www.penguins.org.au
Maru Koala and Animal Park
www.marukoalapark.com.au/
Bendigo
www.bendigotourism.com
Balbirooroo Wetlands
www.visitmorningtonpeninsula.org
Healesville Sanctuary
www.zoo.org.au/healesville
Mornington Peninsula National Park and Bushrangers Bay
www.visitmorningtonpeninsula.org
www.trailhiking.com.au/bushranger-bay-cape-schanck/
Yarra Ranges National Park
www.parkweb.vic.gov.au/explore/parks/yarra-ranges-national-park

Accommodations, Restaurants, and Attractions
www.visitmelbourne.com/Regions/Melbourne/Accommodation
www.hostels.com/melbourne/Australia
www.bestrestaurants.com.au/vic/Melbourne
www.visitvictoria.com/regions/melbourne/things-to-do

Sydney (Warrang)
Transportation
www.opal.com.au
Sydney Visitor Centre
https://visitorcentre.com.au
Sydney Harbour
www.sydney.com/destinations/sydney/sydney-city/sydney-harbour
Sydney Opera House
www.opera.org.au/sydney
Sydney Harbour Bridge
www.bridgeclimb.com
Fort Denison – Muddawahnyuh
https://www.nationalparks.nsw.gov.au/things-to-do/historic-buildings-places/fort-denison-muddawahnyuh
Taronga Zoo
www.taronga.org.au/taronga-zoo
Royal Botanic Garden Sydney
www.rbgsyd.nsw.gov.au
SEA LIFE Sydney Aquarium
www.sydneyaquarium.com.au
Hyde Park
www.cityofsydney.nsw.gov.au/explore/facilities/parks/major-parks/hyde-park
St Mary's Cathedral
www.stmaryscathedral.org.au
Looking to explore the nightlife?
www.sydney.com/things-to-do/night-life/night-clubs
www.nightflow.com/best-nightclubs-in-sydney/

Day Trips from Sydney
www.australia.com/en-us/places/sydney-and-surrounds/best-day-trips.html
www.thecrazytourist.com/15-best-day-trips-sydney/
Manly (Canna)
int.sydney.com/destinations/sydney/sydney-north/manly
Bondi Beach (Boondi)
www.australia.com/en/places/sydney-and-surrounds/locals-guide-to-bondi.html
Australian Reptile Park
www.reptilepark.com.au
Hunter Valley
www.winecountry.com.au
www.huntervalleygardens.com.au
Blue Mountains National Park and Surrounding Area
www.australia.com/en/places/sydney-and-surrounds/guide-to-the-blue-mountains.html

Accommodations, Restaurants, and Attractions
www.sydney.com/accommodation
www.bestrestaurants.com.au/nsw/sydney
www.thecrazytourist.com/25-best-things-sydney-australia/

Cairns (Gimuy)
Transportation
www.cairnsweb.com.au/cairns_transport/getting-around-cairns.asp
Reef Info Visitor Information Centre
tropicalcoasttourism.com.au/see-and-do/information-services/reef-info-visitor-information-centre
The Esplanade
www.cairnsattractions.com.au/explore/family-attractions/cairns-esplanade-lagoon-attractions.395.html
Looking to explore the nightlife?
www.arrivalguides.com/en/Travelguides/Oceania/Australia/Cairns/barsandnightlife

Day Trips from Cairns
www.thecrazytourist.com/15-best-day-trips-from-cairns/
Fitzroy Island (Koba or Gabar)
www.fitzroyislandadventures.com
Cape Tribulation (Kurangee)
www.travelnq.com/things-to-do-in-cape-tribulation/
Daintree
www.destinationdaintree.com/the-daintree/rainforest-reef-rivers-beaches
Skypark Cairns by AJ Hackett
www.skyparkglobal.com/au-en/cairns/activities/bungy
Tully River (Balan Jaban) White Water Rafting
www.ragingthunder.com.au/tully-river-rafting/
Crystal Cascades
www.cairnscanyoning.com

Accommodations, Restaurants, and Attractions
www.australia.com/en-us/places/cairns-and-surrounds/where-to-stay.html
www.hostelworld.com/hostels/Cairns/Australia
www.cairns-australia.com/
www.tropicalnorthqueensland.org.au

Other Places in Australia
Coober Pedy (Umoona)
www.cooberpedy.com
southaustralia.com/destinations/flinders-ranges-and-outback/places/coober-pedy

Alice Springs (Mparntwe)
www.northernterritory.com/us/en/alice-springs-and-surrounds/see-and-do/dining-and-entertainment
www.australia.com/en-us/places/alice-springs-and-surrounds/guide-to-alice-springs.html
www.outback-australia-travel-secrets.com

Darwin (Garramilla)
www.bestrestaurants.com.au/nt/darwin
www.northernterritory.com/darwin-and-surrounds/darwin
www.australia.com/en-us/places/darwin-and-surrounds/guide-to-darwin.html

Perth (Boorloo)
www.bestrestaurants.com.au/wa/perth
www.australia.com/en/places/perth-and-surrounds/guide-to-perth.html
www.experienceperth.com

Adelaide (Tarndanya)
www.bestrestaurants.com.au/sa/adelaide
www.southaustralia.com/places-to-go/adelaide
www.australia.com/en/places/adelaide-and-surrounds.html

Canberra (Ngambri Ngunnawal)
www.bestrestaurants.com.au/act/canberra
www.visitcanberra.com.au

Brisbane (Meanjin)
www.visitbrisbane.com.au

Tasmania (Lutruwita)
www.discovertasmania.com.au

Passport/Visa, Attractions, Culture, and Accommodations
www.australianvisas-eta.com
www.australia.com/en/facts-and-planning/getting-around.html
www.koalanet.com.au/australian-slang.html
www.tripsavvy.com/is-tipping-mandatory-in-australia-1464392
www.roughguides.com/destinations/australasia/australia/accommodation/

NEW ZEALAND (Aotearoa)

Auckland (Tāmaki Makaurau)

Transportation
www.at.govt.nz
i-SITE Visitor Information Centres
www.aucklandnz.com/visit/discover/i-SITE-Visitor-Information-Centres
Sky Tower and SkyCity
www.skycityauckland.co.nz

Auckland War Memorial Museum Tāmaki Paenga Hira
www.aucklandmuseum.com
Maungakiekie / One Tree Hill: Cornwall Park
www.cornwallpark.co.nz/visitor-info
Maungawhau / Mount Eden
www.aucklandnz.com/visit/destinations/auckland-central/mount-eden-and-kingsland

Cathedral of St Patrick & St Joseph
www.stpatricks.org.nz
Auckland Bridge Bungy Jump and Climb
www.bungy.co.nz/auckland/auckland-bridge/
Looking to explore the nightlife?
www.aucklandnz.com/visit/discover/top-10s/top-10-things-to-do-at-night
www.heartofthecity.co.nz/auckland-nightlife/clubs

Day Trips from Auckland
www.experienceoz.com.au/en/best-auckland-day-trips
www.thecrazytourist.com/15-best-day-trips-from-auckland/
Hobbiton
www.hobbitontours.com
www.newzealand.com/int/home-of-middle-earth
Waitakere Ranges Regional Park
www.newzealand.com/us/feature/waitakere-ranges/
Muriwai Beach
www.tourism.net.nz/nz-places/muriwai-beach-new-zealand.html
Piha Beach
www.piha.co.nz

Tiritiri Matangi Open Sanctuary
www.tiritirimatangi.org.nz
Waitomo Caves
www.waitomo.com/Waitomo-Glowworm-Caves/Pages/default.aspx

Accommodations, Restaurants, and Attractions
www.aucklandnz.com/visit/stay
www.aucklandnz.com/visit/taste/best-places-to-eat
www.backpackerboard.co.nz/hostels/auckland-hostels/

Other Places in New Zealand: North Island (Te Ika-a-Māui) & South Island (Te Waipounamu)

Wellington (Te Whanganui-a-Tara), North Island
www.wellingtonnz.com
Tauranga, North Island
www.downtowntauranga.co.nz
www.newzealand.com/int/tauranga
Taupō, North Island
www.greatlaketaupo.com
www.newzealand.com/int/taupo
Rotorua, North Island
www.rotoruanz.com
www.tepuia.com
Napier (Ahuriri), North Island
www.newzealand.com/us/napier/
Christchurch (Ōtautahi), South Island
www.christchurchnz.com
Queenstown (Tāhuna), South Island
www.queenstownnz.co.nz
Dunedin (Ōtepoti), South Island
www.visit-newzealand.co.nz/Dunedin

Passport/Visa, Attractions, Culture, and Accommodations
www.immigration.govt.nz/new-zealand-visas/apply-for-a-visa/tools-and-information/
www.mustdonewzealand.co.nz/south-island-new-zealand-things-to-do
www.newzealandslang.com
www.newzealand.com/us/bed-and-breakfast
www.hostels.com/new-zealand

FIJI

The Official Website of Tourism, Fiji
www.fiji.travel
Fiji Accommodations
www.tourismfiji.com
www.beachcomberfiji.com
Transportation
fijipocketguide.com/public-transport-in-fiji/
Passport/Visa, Attractions, Culture, and Accommodations
www.worldtravelguide.net/guides/oceania/fiji/passport-visa
www.travelandleisure.com/travel-guide/fiji
www.fijiislands.com.au/fiji-travel-advice/

About the Author

Caitlyn M. Schmidt lives in the Seattle, Washington area. She graduated with honors from Western Washington University, where she earned a Bachelor of Arts in English with an Emphasis on Creative Writing.

Mrs. Schmidt has visited numerous countries across six continents on trips with both family and friends. Her love of travel and world cultures inspired her to write *Fun Down Under.*

www.ingramcontent.com/pod-product-compliance
Lightning Source LLC
LaVergne TN
LVHW072326090426
835512LV00031B/10